Madonna of the Cat

Madonna of the Cat

Sue Mach

SHANGANA PRESS

Published by
Shangana Press
Portland, Oregon, USA
shanganapress.com

ISBN: 979-8-9871359-6-9 (paperback)
ISBN: 979-8-9871359-7-6 (eBook)

0 9 8 7 6 5 4 3 2

for Bruce

Characters:

HERMIONE, *Queen of Sicilia, presumed dead*
PAULINA, *Hermione's friend*
DONNA, *A Shepherdess in Bohemia*
PERDITA, *The Lost Child of Queen Hermione and King Leontes*
THE BEAR

Madonna of the Cat was first presented at 21ten Theatre, Portland, Oregon, on November 1, 2025, with the following cast and creative team:

Directed by Gemma Whelan

HERMIONE	Crystal Ann Muñoz
PAULINA	Maria Porter
DONNA	Luisa Sermol
PERDITA	Emma Greene
THE BEAR	Bruce Burkhartsmeier
Scenic Designer	Alex Meyer
Costume Designer	Janelle Sutton
Lighting Designer	Sophina Flores
Sound Designer	Lawrence Siulagi
Composer	Stephanie Schneiderman
Props Designer	Skylar Vayda
Movement Director	Adam Fleming
Stage Manager	Ava Violet Schmidt

AUTHOR'S NOTES:

In Shakespeare's *The Winter's Tale* (1610), the first part of which reads like myth, and the second part like a fairy tale, the safety and livelihoods of women are dependent upon men, yet family lineage is reliant upon a woman's act of giving birth, and the one thing men can't control is the certainty of paternity. "No barricado for a belly," (1.2.253) rages King Leontes, whose obsessive jealousy drives him to believe his best friend Polixenes has impregnated his wife, Hermione. Subsequently, he imprisons her, declares her a whore, then subjects her to a humiliating public trial. Her fate is dependent upon an oracle handed down by Apollo, who pronounces her innocent and her baby "legitimate." Still, Leontes' fury results in the death of his only son, the casting out into the wilderness of his infant daughter Perdita, and the collapse of Hermione—presumed dead at the end of Act III. Apollo warns the chastened and repentant Leontes that he will have no heir "if that which is lost be not found," (3.2.145).

Sixteen years pass between the first part of the play and Act IV, which features growth, rebirth, and Perdita's coming of age. It also includes Shakespeare's most famous stage direction, "Exit, pursued by a bear." In the end we learn Hermione is not dead, but has been sequestered with her friend Paulina for sixteen years while Bohemian shepherds raised her daughter. *Madonna of the Cat* imagines those lost years, examining themes of friendship, motherhood, and forgiveness.

Another relevant aspect of this story is its mention of the only artist to whom Shakespeare ever refers directly in his work, Giulio Romano (1499–1546). Romano was an acolyte of Raphael and painted a number of Madonna and Child portraits. One of Romano's works lends its name to this play.

PROLOGUE

In the dark, a woman is humming something like a lullaby. As the lights come up, we see that it's **PAULINA**. She has a cold compress and is wiping the forehead of an unconscious woman as she sings. The only furnishings in the room are a bed and a wooden stove for heat. The only window is a skylight. The woman in the bed is **HERMIONE**. **PAULINA** continues to wipe **HERMIONE'S** arms and legs. Eventually, she tucks her back in bed, takes a last look at her and exits. Black out. MUSIC.

SCENE I

(Lights up in the same room in PAULINA'S house. Time has passed. HERMIONE wakes up startled, as if from a bad dream. She puts her arms across her breasts and doubles over in pain. She touches her neck. She hears the sound of a heavy metal door slamming, and then footsteps. She pulls the covers over her head. She waits. She gets up and goes to the door. She tries to open it. She knocks on it. She waits. She goes back to the bed and waits for a moment. She gets up again and goes to the door. She knocks more forcefully and pulls on the door handle. No response. Her knocks become more frantic.)

HERMIONE: Out. Out. OUT!!!

(The door pushes open. PAULINA enters. HERMIONE retreats to the bed.)

PAULINA: SHHH—

HERMIONE: Paulina—

PAULINA: Quiet—we need to be—

HERMIONE: I'm dead.

PAULINA: SHHH—

HERMIONE: I'm dead.

PAULINA: No—

HERMIONE: What have you done?

PAULINA: Speak softly.

HERMIONE: What have you done??!!!!

(HERMIONE puts her arms across her breasts and doubles over in pain.)

PAULINA: SHHHH. I saw you breathing.

HERMIONE: I would've stopped—

PAULINA: No—

HERMIONE: My milk—

PAULINA: I know—

HERMIONE: It hurts.

PAULINA: I know. I brought you tea. (She feels **HERM-IONE'S** forehead.) Your fever's broken. Drink the tea.

HERMIONE: No.

PAULINA: It will help with the pain.

HERMIONE: Let me die.

PAULINA: (Ignoring her, indicating the fire.) I've tried to keep the room warm. You need a proper bath.

HERMIONE: What have you done?

PAULINA: I don't know.

HERMIONE: How long have I been here?

PAULINA: A day. Almost two. Maybe more. (She indicates under the bed.) There's a bedpan.

HERMIONE: I saw Mamillius—in a dream? He—he—we were playing a game in the rose garden. He cut his finger on a thorn and the blood wouldn't stop. *Mother*—he said—no, he asked it like a question. I wrapped his hand in my skirt—and the blood wouldn't stop.

PAULINA: What do you remember?

HERMIONE: He's dead—or did I dream it?

PAULINA: No. (Pause.) Your son is dead.

HERMIONE: And my baby—is she—

PAULINA: She'll live.

HERMIONE: How do you know?

PAULINA: You smell like sour milk.

(**HERMIONE** smells herself. She laughs a little. Then she begins to cry.)

HERMIONE: Does anybody else know?

PAULINA: We'll bury you tomorrow.

HERMIONE: Then convent?

PAULINA: You'll stay here.

HERMIONE: Or brothel—*whore*—I can't stay here.

PAULINA: You can't leave. I've created a bit of a dilemma.

HERMIONE: How long?

PAULINA: I don't know.

HERMIONE: It hurts.

PAULINA: The milk will dry.

HERMIONE: I got to nurse her for a day—hold her against my skin—and then you took her.

PAULINA: To be fair—

HERMIONE: You did—you—

PAULINA: We're trying to save her.

HERMIONE: We?

PAULINA: Antigonus took the baby.

HERMIONE: How can she live?

PAULINA: We have to wait. (Examining **HERMIONE**.) Somehow, you've scraped your neck. I'll bring a salve.

(**HERMIONE** puts her hand to her neck. There is the sound of a metal door slamming and footsteps.)

HERMIONE: Someone else is here—

PAULINA: No one—

HERMIONE: I thought I heard—

PAULINA: Whatever you were dreaming might still be in your head.

HERMIONE: How can she live?

PAULINA: Linens, a charm—a piece of lace that smells like you. I prepared a box for her.

HERMIONE: You don't know that she's alive.

PAULINA: She's with Antigonus.

HERMIONE: I need to see her—

(HERMIONE goes to the door. PAULINA stops
her and holds her back.)

PAULINA: Forgive me, but you can't.

HERMIONE: Why?

PAULINA: What do you remember?

HERMIONE: My face—only it wasn't me—on every post— *whore*—and it was me—and we were—the floor was hard and Emilia found a blanket—such a small comfort—

PAULINA: Do you remember the trial?

HERMIONE: The oracle—Apollo's—the oracle. Innocent.

PAULINA: The word was chaste—

HERMIONE: I only did what Leontes asked me to.

PAULINA: I know.

HERMIONE: I only—

PAULINA: *Leontes is a jealous tyrant; his innocent babe truly begotten; and the king shall live without an heir if that which is lost be not found.* It's etched in my brain—the oracle.

HERMIONE: In that brief moment after I heard it, I was so relieved. For one breath. And then—I don't understand why my boy had to die. He liked the feel of velvet and the way the light would create a shadow through the trees when the sun was setting. He wasn't meant for this kind of world. It wasn't very specific—the oracle—

PAULINA: No . . .

HERMIONE: . . . nothing about me living.

PAULINA: I made a choice.

HERMIONE: Not a favorable move in this climate.

PAULINA: I'm not sure what I've done. The doctor placed a feather on your lips—nothing. We all thought you were dead. Oh, the fire that was in me when I thought he took you. It was my heart—certainly not my head—that led me back into that court. And my rage. I couldn't stop him from breaking your son's heart to the point of death. And I couldn't stop him from casting forth your daughter to whatever wildness may find her. But you? I believed the strength of your honor would somehow bring us back to what we once were. So, to take you? I stood in the shadow of his bottomless need, and I cursed him with everything in me. I was bold. And the strange thing is he took in my words like an embrace that grabs breath. He commended me for my truth. Now, for better or for worse, he and I are intertwined like two drowning swimmers trying to surface as we find out what Fortune has in store for us. (Pause.) You were laid beside your boy—

HERMIONE: I remember—

PAULINA: —and Leontes came in to see but he was too afraid to touch you. He told me to prepare you both—to be—to be buried.

HERMIONE: You dressed my boy—

PAULINA: —but I saw you breathing. So I sculpted a body— your burial body—and I brought you here in the wagon I use for gardening.

HERMIONE: You put me in a wagon?

PAULINA: It wasn't a rational decision.

HERMIONE: (Pause.) What happens next?

PAULINA: I don't know.

HERMIONE: *There was a man—dwelt by a churchyard.* That's how Mamillius began his story—the last time we were in the garden. In my dream I saw him bleeding and I couldn't make it stop. I can't do anything.

PAULINA: You will. We will—

HERMIONE: We will what?

PAULINA: I'm not sure. We have to wait for them.

HERMIONE: Who?

PAULINA: The baby. Antigonus. I saw you breathing.

HERMIONE: I want to hold her.

PAULINA: Then wait with me. Who else have you got?

> (**HERMIONE** holds her breasts. She doubles over in pain. Lights fade on **HERMIONE** and **PAULINA**.)

SCENE II

(Lights go up on **DONNA** in Bohemia. She is
nursing a baby. She doubles over in pain.)

DONNA: Bloody Hell!!

(The baby begins to cry.)

Shhhh little one. I don't mean to carry on so. I'm trying as
best I can, but you're sucking the life out of me. Not that I
have much left to give. (She talks to the baby.) You're a wee
mystery, aren't you? Ah. That's all right then. We'll take you
as you are. You know, my sister Miriam—she was a nurse-
maid for the queen. The future king—unless he mucks it
up—he gnawed on her for quite some time until he started
to get teeth. Miriam is the one who told me that a woman
can get milk to come even after she's past the bleeding
stage. (She tries to nurse again and winces in pain.) Bloody
full of it, she is. Ah. It feels like someone's taking a knife to
my nipple from the inside.

(The baby begins to cry.)

Shhh little one. *Perdita.* That's what the note says to call
you. *Perdita.* What kind of name is that? I wanted to
change it to Elsie, but the old man says keep what's written. It's meant to be. All this has a hint of something sinis-
ter if you ask me—what with that gentleman who left you
getting *pursued* and *eaten* by a bear. That's a new one on
me. *Speaking of gnawing.* I've got to wash blood from all
your belongings before anyone suspects something strange
of us. (She pulls **PERDITA** away.) I'm sorry. I have nothing
to give and my titties are all worn down.

(**PERDITA** cries. **DONNA** stands up and begins
to rock her.)

Shhh.

> (She begins to sing.)

Where did you come from pretty Perdita?
A woman's mistake?
A rich man's rape?
Stair work, floor work, behind-the-door work—

What brought you to my arms, pretty Perdita?
Was there fire in your making?
Or blood in the taking of a woman's worth?
Clean work, mean work, or act of love work—

It doesn't matter pretty little Perdita
You're mine today
We'll sing, we'll play—I'll keep the wolves at bay.
Barn work, charm work, queen of the farm work.

You'll know love
You'll know love
You'll know love.

(Speaking.) There now. Are you sleeping then? Good. Give
an old woman some rest.

> (She sets the baby down gingerly and goes to
> the cabinet to pour herself a drink.)

I believe I've earned this.

> (She sits still for a moment, just looking at
> the baby. She speaks to it.)

You know what else my sister tells me? The king—what do
they call him? *Polixenes.* He arrived back here in Bohemia
after a mighty falling out with his friend Leontes over in
Sicilia. Who bestows these royals with such phony names,
huh? Most likely one or the other of them jumped the back
fence—tasted the fruit of another man's orchard if you

know what I mean. Maybe you're connected to all of it but I'm going to stuff that thought—never speak of it. (Pause.) I'm not his real wife—now I'm talking about the old coot who found you. His wife died years ago—birthing his son who I suppose is now your brother? Imagine that! It'll all make sense one day. Anyway. Here I am once more—keeping a wee thing alive. I'll do better this time around. If we spend what you came with, they'll arrest us for thievery—that's what I tell the old man. He says we'll use the money slowly over time—and most folks will think we've just done well with our sheep. Only no one does well with sheep. He says we're blessed by the fairies, but I don't know. Maybe you'll be the death of us.

(**PERDITA** begins to cry again.)

DONNA: Bloody hell!!

(She picks up the baby and rocks it while she hums a lullaby. MUSIC. A bear enters and sits on a rock outside **DONNA'S** house.)

BEAR: I did not pursue the man. He woke me up from a dead winter's sleep. Thought he could just drop a fucking baby in the woods and LEAVE. (Pause.) Bears don't *pursue*. He trespassed through my critical area—everyone's got one—woke me up before it was time to wake up. And I—I—I don't know. I would've behaved more nobly—especially considering the man left a noble's kid—who I might've passed over for the wolves to take care of—if I wanted to. But. See. The man started waving his arms and running towards me—attempting to throw me off my game. The wanker! I suppose I could've just walked away. But—I—everything was off. Hard to explain. You know, I am pretty much accepting of folks most of the time. You wanna prance around in your cap and your feathers—who am I to say? But what irks me is that stupid fuck wouldn't survive five minutes in the woods. Thinks he can just waltz on in here and drop a baby when IT'S NOT HIS CRITICAL AREA! So. I devoured him—just went for the limbs like you would a turkey leg. But I didn't pursue. He came to me. And I'm here to tell you—the gods were urging me on and I just ingested him. And now I'm relegated to a fucking stage direction for all eternity. Do you know how humiliating this is? I don't pursue. I defend what's mine—couple of cubs in the cave up a way—they're not mine per se, but their mom and me meet end to end from time to time—so what. And the sky! You should've seen it. Like a—like a shroud it was. But then these streaks of light cutting through like veins. And the sea rose up like a massive fucking hand. And yes, there's a sea coast in Bohemia, GET OVER IT! Anyway, I devoured the man and the long and short of it is I've got an ache in my belly and I'm asking you not to judge me—I'm only hu—no. I'M A BEAR!! Ursa fucking Major. And I would like you to respect my dignity, and perhaps join me in my quest to remove the word pursue from subsequent editions of the text of this tale. Thank you.

> (The **BEAR** exits, pursuing no one. **DONNA**
> rocks **PERDITA** to sleep. MUSIC.)

DONNA:

Monkshood, crab apple, apricot, ash,
Bachelor's button, barley, woodbine dash.
Learn these roots in your dreams little one.
They'll be in your bones with the rise of the sun.

Ginger, gooseberry, lady-smock, lark's heel,
Pignut, pomegranate, rosemary, chamomile.

Learn what to eat, learn what not.
Mind the sick, you're all they've got.

Oh, pretty Perdita,
With the silver spoon,
I'll show you the forest in June.

Dirt work, earth work, queen of the hearth work,

You'll know love
You'll know love
You'll know love.

(Lights fade on **DONNA**.)

SCENE III

(A few months later. **HERMIONE** stands under the skylight in her room, taking in the light. **PAULINA** enters, dragging a desk. She proceeds to set it up for **HERMIONE**.)

PAULINA: I've brought paper and ink, like you asked.

HERMIONE: (Taking in the desk and the writing utensils.) Thank you.

PAULINA: I have to do the washing myself.

HERMIONE: So?

PAULINA: Try not to make a mess. Please.

HERMIONE: I'm not a child.

(**PAULINA** notices **HERMIONE'S** neck.)

PAULINA: You're healing.

(**HERMIONE** touches her neck. She hears the sound of a door slamming.)

HERMIONE: Is someone else here?

PAULINA: No one. Are you hungry?

HERMIONE: No.

PAULINA: You need to eat.

HERMIONE: I'm not hungry.

PAULINA: (Pause.) I saw him—Leontes—at the churchyard—beside your grave.

HERMIONE: *There was a man dwelt by the churchyard. . .*

PAULINA: He goes every day. I wasn't going to tell you, but who else can I tell? He looked so small. I stood there—prepared to drop my flowers on the dirt—it's almost impossible to look at him. I tried to turn away. *Stay.* He said. And I—suddenly my feet were rooted. I couldn't move, and he wouldn't look at me. How many months? he asked me. I said I was losing track but it's not yet been a year because we haven't seen summer. The ship is lost, he said.

HERMIONE: The one that took her? Lost?

PAULINA: Everyone on it—a storm—

HERMIONE: They're all gone?

PAULINA: They were coming home from wherever he left her.

HERMIONE: Antigonus?

PAULINA: My husband is gone. I'm trying to get used to saying it.

HERMIONE: (Pause.) I'm sorry.

PAULINA: I'm not sure what I've done. Or what I've been called on to do.

> (HERMIONE reaches out her hand. PAULINA takes it. They sit for a moment.)

HERMIONE: What if we left?

PAULINA: From here? We certainly can't—I can't imagine. . .

HERMIONE: We could—

PAULINA: What?

HERMIONE: . . .No. There's really no way out is there?

> (PAULINA is silent.)

HERMIONE: Then we'll keep waiting.

> (PAULINA lets go of HERMIONE'S hand. She exits. HERMIONE paces. Then she sits. She dips her pen in ink and begins to write.)

HERMIONE: To my dearest Perdita—wherever you are—if indeed you *are*. Perhaps you're just as surprised by an intake of breath as I am. How easily it can be taken from us. How readily it fills a room. (She breathes.) The act of being born is, well—one of violence. But the fact that one comes into this world at all—that's beauty. Believing in the beauty of you is what will root me here. I'm writing to remember what happened. (She touches her neck.) So much of it I can't—it's like I'm squinting to see. A man has died so you can live. And you had a brother, Mamillius. You would've liked him very much. He was soft, and when he hurt himself he would bleed and bleed.

(MUSIC. Lights fade on **HERMIONE** as she continues writing.)

SCENE IV

(We hear the humming of a child in the darkness. Lights up on **PERDITA** in Bohemia. She is now around five years old. She and the **BEAR** toss a ball to one another inside **DONNA'S** house. **PERDITA** puts down her ball, retrieves **DONNA'S** bonnet and apron and puts them on the **BEAR**, who sits very still.)

PERDITA: I'll be right back.

(While **PERDITA** is out of the room, the **BEAR** finds **DONNA'S** liquor. He takes a swig from the bottle.)

BEAR: What's this? (He takes another swig.) Nectar of the gods.

(He puts the bottle back and quickly assumes his previous stillness as **PERDITA** returns, carrying a tea set.)

PERDITA: The tea is ready. I am so delighted to see you.

(**PERDITA** pours pretend tea for the **BEAR** and for herself. They hold their pinkies out and drink like royalty. **DONNA** calls from outside.)

DONNA: (Offstage.) PEERRDDITTTA!!!!!

PERDITA: I'm afraid I have to go now.

DONNA: PEERRDDITTTA!!!!! Come get clean!

PERDITA: I'm five today. We're having a picnic. I wish you could join us.

DONNA: PEERRDDITTTA!!!!!

PERDITA: COMING!!! (To the **BEAR**.) I had a lovely afternoon, and I do hope you come again soon.

(The **BEAR** nods his head but remains mostly
still. **PERDITA** removes the bonnet and apron
from him, hangs it up and exits. MUSIC.
Lights up on **HERMIONE** in her room. There
is a pile of undelivered letters to **PERDITA**.
The desk is covered with a beautiful lace
cloth. She writes.)

HERMIONE: When I can sleep—which is rare—upon wak-
ing I experience a glorious moment that belongs to a time
before I forgot what time is. Oh, my dearest Perdita, if that
moment were real, this might be the morning we're pre-
paring for our portrait. You would bring me a sash and
I would tie it around your crisp lace dress. Your *stiff* lace
dress. In our glimmering white gowns—our spotless white
gowns, splashed with ribbons of color, we would make our
way to a room of light where a famous painter is waiting.
And we would sit on a velvet chaise—spines straight, hands
still. You'd try and run, and I'd urge you to stop moving . . .

(The **BEAR**, alone in **DONNA'S** empty house,
rummages through the garbage. **PERDITA**
enters the room and gleefully joins the
BEAR in his rummaging, then quickly exits.
HERMIONE continues to write.)

HERMIONE: And later, once I saw the portrait—you and I
in the perfect pose—our porcelain skin catching the light
just so—I'm afraid what I would most likely see are two
ghosts. As if I'm looking back from a future in which we
have ceased to be.

BEAR: (To the audience as **HERMIONE** continues to write.)
Do you know where the term "licked into shape" comes
from? Bears. You see, when a cub enters the world it squirts
out in one big blob, coated in some blob-like substance.

Then the mother licks and licks and licks the blob into a wee bear form. It's all done very affectionately. It's your lot that's bastardized the term—*licked into shape.* Just for future reference. (Pause.) If you know this story—this *Winter's Tale,* you'll know that Time is a character—designed to be poetical or maybe I should say metaphorical—meaning he's a fucking device used to move the plot along. But, see, TIME CAME INTO MY CRITICAL AREA. So. I have taken on the role of time, and time is in me. (He burps.) So. From here on out the minutes, hours, days—fuck that shit. One can mark one's aging by the drip drip drip of the rain.

(MUSIC. The **BEAR** takes one more swig of liquor, tops off the bottle with a little water, replaces it. **HERMIONE'S** skylight begins to leak. She puts her hand up and feels the rain. She twirls around in it at the same time the **BEAR** twirls around in **DONNA'S** house. **HERMIONE** returns to her desk. The **BEAR** exits.)

SCENE V

(PAULINA enters HERMIONE'S room carrying something enormous that's wrapped in paper.)

PAULINA: (Out of breath.) I did something extraordinary today.

(PAULINA notices the water. HERMIONE doesn't respond. She is writing. PAULINA nonchalantly attempts to peek at HERMIONE'S writing. HERMIONE blocks her view.)

PAULINA: How long has the rain—

HERMIONE: Not very long.

PAULINA: You'll catch your death—

HERMIONE: If Apollo has spared me this long, I don't think the rain will kill me.

(PAULINA leans the painting against the wall, takes one of HERMIONE'S towels and wipes up the water. She puts a bowl down to catch the water.)

PAULINA: That will do for now. You're not going to ask me about —

HERMIONE: (She notices the painting.) It's almost bigger than you are.

PAULINA: I made a *purchase*. It's for you.

(HERMIONE regards the wrapped painting, but she doesn't open it.)

PAULINA: Don't just stare at it.

(HERMIONE tears the paper off of the painting. She takes it in. It's like nothing she has ever seen.)

HERMIONE: Who are they?

PAULINA: I don't know. The artist is Giulio Romano.

HERMIONE: Who?

PAULINA: That's what the man who sold it to me said—

HERMIONE: The man who sold—

PAULINA: I made a purchase!

HERMIONE: Giulio Romano.

PAULINA: He's from Rome.

HERMIONE: Does that explain him?

PAULINA: The painting has a title—*Madonna of the Cat*.

HERMIONE: What's a Madonna?

PAULINA: I don't know.

HERMIONE: The painting has a title?

PAULINA: Fascinating, yes?

HERMIONE: I see it there—the cat. It's looking at us. None of the others are.

(HERMIONE goes to the painting and touches it.)

HERMIONE: (Looking at the painting.) A mother and two children.

PAULINA: Yes.

HERMIONE: Are these strangers from the past or future? And the woman has a friend.

PAULINA: They reminded me of a certain comfort we had once. See the sewing in the basket there? It seems they're from some world outside of ours, and I fear Apollo might strike me down just for looking at them, but here they are.

I should get rid of it. Somehow, I thought you'd like the colors. I didn't mean to be insensitive — with the children – in the moment I thought—I'll take it away.

HERMIONE: (Indicating the painting.) The child here is Cupid, yes?

PAULINA: I didn't think of that.

HERMIONE: We'll call him Cupid. (She studies the painting.) They all seem so ordinary—so—natural—

PAULINA: Except they have golden rings of light coming from their heads.

HERMIONE: Wouldn't it be something if we all had a golden ring of light coming from our heads?

PAULINA: Perhaps we do and fail to recognize it.

HERMIONE: Blasphemous!

(Suddenly they both begin to laugh. HERMIONE goes to the painting again.)

PAULINA: It's strange how no one creates anymore. At least not in public. It's not an official ban, yet it seems no one dares add color to our collective palette. I had to go somewhat underground to make this *purchase*—

HERMIONE: There's a man lurking in the doorway.

PAULINA: I wouldn't necessarily refer to it as lurking—

HERMIONE: What does he want from them?

PAULINA: I should take it away.

HERMIONE: Leave it—please. (Pause.) Thank you for thinking of me.

(PAULINA starts to leave, but turns back.)

PAULINA: It feels like so much fog—the kind where you can't see what's in front of you—all this waiting. (Referring to the painting.) And so I grab pieces of comfort.

HERMIONE: Who wouldn't?

PAULINA: (Pause.) Leontes has finally begun tending to your garden—at least part of it. I think he believed if we left it untouched it would never change. But it's grown wild in five years—so he's having it cleared and pruned and—I don't know—structured. In the middle he's building a monument.

HERMIONE: A monument?

PAULINA: To you. It will be glorious.

HERMIONE: Me?

PAULINA: Finest craftsmen—no expense spared—

HERMIONE: I—I don't want a monument.

PAULINA: So in generations to come, no one will forget you. It will take years to complete.

HERMIONE: A waste—

PAULINA: Not for him—or me.

HERMIONE: Comfort.

PAULINA: Yes, comfort. I have committed to helping him craft something for the ages.

> (HERMIONE goes to the painting and touches it.)

HERMIONE: The man in the doorway never makes it into the room.

> (Water begins to drip from the skylight again. PAULINA watches it.)

PAULINA: You're going to have to move.

HERMIONE: Can I go outside?

PAULINA: Of course not—

HERMIONE: The moon is full. Take me outside.

PAULINA: I—

HERMIONE: Please?

PAULINA: Tomorrow.

HERMIONE: You say that every time I ask. Promise.

PAULINA: I can fix the skylight myself.

HERMIONE: I like to feel the rain. Find me a cat.

PAULINA: No.

HERMIONE: At least you didn't promise. (Pause.) What happens next?

PAULINA: I don't know. I don't like my dreams when the moon is full.

> (**PAULINA** exits. **HERMIONE** begins a new page of writing.)

HERMIONE: My dearest Perdita. Are you somewhere under this moon that's showing off a circle of golden light? You would look positively ethereal underneath it. Maybe I could fade into it—your light. I believe if you were here tomorrow, I'd begin teaching you how to dance. It would be awkward at first, but it's never too early to begin.

> (MUSIC. Lights up on **PERDITA** and the **BEAR** waltzing under the moonlight. **PERDITA** is a little older, maybe six or seven. She stands on the **BEAR'S** feet. In her room, **HERMIONE** briefly waltzes with a pretend partner. Then she returns to her desk.)

HERMIONE: I received a gift today—a painting. It tells a story of two ordinary women and a cat. Oh, and there's a man lurking in the doorway and children who look like little gods. And there are so many other things to discover. I don't quite know what the story is yet. I've got plenty of time to craft a plot. I wish you were here to help me figure it out.

(Lights fade on **HERMIONE**. **PERDITA** and the **BEAR** bow to one another.)

SCENE VI

(**DONNA** enters with a bucket of flowers.)

DONNA: PERDITA!!!!

(The **BEAR** and **PERDITA** exit quickly.)

PERDITA: Coming!!!

DONNA: You best be bringing water.

(**PERDITA** enters with water.)

DONNA: Are you trying to murder your flowers? Don't leave them sitting dry. Here.

(**DONNA** gives **PERDITA** some scissors.)

Trim them up and I'll tell you the names.

(**PERDITA** takes a flower from the bucket. She snips off the end and puts it water. She continues to do this with each choice.)

DONNA: Eryngoes. Be careful with that one. It's prickly.

PERDITA: This one.

DONNA: That's gooseberry—another one that will stick you if you're not careful. Show me your hands.

(**PERDITA** does so.)

Ah. I don't know how you manage to keep your fingers so clean. That will change when we start going after roots. This berry's not quite ripe. You have to pick them at the right moment. After that, we'll make the best pie you've ever tasted. I'll show you. That's essential, you know—the right moment. Because the harvest doesn't wait for you. What else have you got?

PERDITA: These.

DONNA: Ah. Flax.

PERDITA: I think they're beautiful.

DONNA: Useful too. You make linen from the fiber in flax. It's not an easy thing to do. Rich folks like linen.

PERDITA: Are we rich?

DONNA: Ha!

PERDITA: What do you mean by Ha!?

DONNA: We have enough. How about that?

PERDITA: That's not a very good answer. What are you doing?

> (DONNA has been making a flower crown from the flax.)

DONNA: I made you a wee crown. Hold still and let me coronate you. There now. You're a princess.

PERDITA: Am I rich?

DONNA: You're glorious.

PERDITA: Can I wear linen?

DONNA: You can wear whatever you like.

PERDITA: I can?

DONNA: Absolutely. And you get to boss everyone around.

PERDITA: Everyone?

DONNA: Except maybe your man, whoever that might be. They tend to take over.

PERDITA: Not me.

DONNA: We'll see. What would you do on your first day of rule?

PERDITA: Everyone will pick flowers.

DONNA: Excellent idea, your majesty.

PERDITA: And there will be dancing.

DONNA: Wonderful. And singing?

PERDITA: Only by people who know how to sing.

DONNA: And those that don't?

PERDITA: Off with their heads!

DONNA: Oh my. Grandma Donna's pipes are a wee bit rusty. What will you do with me?

PERDITA: You can fix my hair and make me pie.

DONNA: But you'd spare me head?

PERDITA: Of course.

DONNA: And you wouldn't really be a beast to those who gave everything to look after you, would you?

PERDITA: You'd have *my* head.

DONNA: I would indeed.

PERDITA: If I was a princess, does that mean my mother would come back?

DONNA: I wish that could be so for your sake. Although I'd be sure to miss you.

PERDITA: Tell me again how I lost her.

DONNA: Well there was this bear—came upon her—pursued her out of season and out of nowhere.

PERDITA: I have a bear.

DONNA: Do you now?

PERDITA: He's a gentleman, and he lets me boss him around.

DONNA: Well this bear certainly was not a gentleman. We had to run him off.

PERDITA: Hmm. Why?

DONNA: Why? He came into our critical area!! No more yammering. Let's get out to the garden before the rain.

(The sound of distant thunder. **DONNA, PER-DITA** exit. MUSIC. The **BEAR** enters. He has insomnia and has gained weight.)

BEAR: Perfidy. Mendacity. And Bullshit. *Run me off!* (Pause.) I admit I've become a bit attached to the little one. I know what you're thinking. I promise not to devour her. In fact, I feel the need to—I don't know—someone's got to look after her. (Pause.) I can't sleep—which is not according to plan. And I know what you're thinking. Oh, he's gained weight. IT'S A NATURAL FUCKING OCCURRENCE! I'm supposed to be slumbering blissfully through the winter, but look at me standing here—pleading with you. It's all quite perturbing. And I've never uttered the word perturbing before. I ask you this: Who's pursuing who? Or whom? Fuck!

> (The **BEAR** goes to **DONNA'S** kitchen, takes an entire bottle of liquor, and exits. Lights fade. MUSIC.)

SCENE VII

(Lights up on **HERMIONE**, standing under
her skylight. More paintings of the Madonna and Child by various artists hang about
the room. A few are leaned against the wall.
Madonna of the Cat is the largest piece of art
and still the central focus. **HERMIONE** reach-
es up to feel for rain leaking through the skylight. There is none. She returns to her desk
and takes out paper.)

HERMIONE: If I am tracking the time correctly—and that
may be questionable—but if I am, you are ten today,
Perdita. It's a year your dance becomes less free. A pat-
tern will begin to form. Spine straight, hand out, touching
another, then turning away. It takes several years to learn. I
wonder if you ever will.

(MUSIC. Lights up on **PERDITA** and the
BEAR doing a "proper" waltz in the dishev-
eled household. At the end of the dance she
pushes him away. Lights fade.)

HERMIONE: (Still writing.) The rain has been glorious to
me. For three changes of the seasons, it crept in through
the skylight until finally Paulina had to move me. She
had to face the fact that she couldn't fix the leak herself. I
went outside in the dark and consumed the night air like
so much cake. I've been going out ever since—just for a
while—that's a secret between us. Paulina and I had to hide
the paintings. I'm so relieved to have them back.

(**PAULINA** enters.)

PAULINA: I've brought some linens.

(**PAULINA** places the linens on the bed. She tries to take a sneaky peek at **HERMIONE'S** writing. **HERMIONE** blocks her from doing so.)

HERMIONE: Thank you.

PAULINA: (Looking up at the skylight.) It looks like the seal is holding.

HERMIONE: It is. (Referring to *Madonna of the Cat*) And it feels so much better now that we've hung this properly.

PAULINA: It does.

HERMIONE: I miss the rain.

PAULINA: I decidedly do not.

HERMIONE: I've begun praying.

PAULINA: To Apollo—

HERMIONE: To Artemis. I want to be something else. A tree—like Daphne. I would never have to come inside.

PAULINA: People are saying—they say your ghost haunts the orchard.

HERMIONE: It does.

PAULINA: If you're caught—

HERMIONE: I won't get caught.

PAULINA: Please stop.

HERMIONE: People take what they can find in the orchard. In complete darkness! There are so many things I didn't notice before—before I died. I always thought of trees as having roots. Now I imagine them holding up the sky. And do you know there are people—*ordinary people*—who read the stars? I want to learn how. And one time—one time an elegant old woman gave me her best apple because she thought I needed it. She put her hand on top of mine. It was the warmest touch I've ever had.

PAULINA: If they find you—

HERMIONE: They won't find me—

PAULINA: You can't predict. And perhaps you should take a moment to think about—to think—never mind.

HERMIONE: To think about?

PAULINA: Us.

HERMIONE: Us?

PAULINA: The rest of us. Never mind.

HERMIONE: I've ventured as far as the edge of the garden. Sometimes I think I might see my son's ghost there, and we could play games like we used to. And maybe he would tell me a story. Last night I stood under his window—Leontes—

PAULINA: Tell me you only dreamed that—

HERMIONE: He was writing, and I was curious—I've never seen him so focused before—so intent. I had to fight the urge to go inside—as if I'd just been out a moment—and ask him what—what would I ask him?

PAULINA: They brought in a woman from Spain.

HERMIONE: A woman?

PAULINA: I told myself I wouldn't tell you—but who else can I tell? There's pressure—ten years is a long time to wait. And they fear our Sicilia is no longer stable.

HERMIONE: They?

PAULINA: So many people you used to know are gone now. There's a new *they*. She was young—

HERMIONE: Young—

PAULINA: Well yes—

HERMIONE: And luminous—worthy of a thousand stories—

PAULINA: Let me finish. Her father made a generous offer. There was a lot of—it could have been a beneficial coupling—land. Assets. Safety. But—

HERMIONE: Gifts were exchanged. A banquet—

PAULINA: —well it was unlike any I'd seen since, since—

HERMIONE: Before—

PAULINA: You died. Yes. I was beginning to panic. Leontes was gracious. There was something of a spark of the old—I saw him *laugh*. I didn't know what I'd do if, if some kind of arrangement, or agreement—but—

HERMIONE: But?

PAULINA: They finally brought this young woman into the banquet hall—Isabelle—she looked so frightened. And when he saw her, he began—I thought he was laughing at first—but they were sobs. Cries from so deep—and he couldn't stop. Everyone stood there—silent—and the breath and the choking—finally I went to him. Someone—I don't even remember who—shuffled the guests into another room. We sat on the floor.

HERMIONE: You sat on the floor?

PAULINA: I rocked him like a baby, and do you know what he finally said? He said—*never forget to remind me what I'm capable of.*

HERMIONE: (Pause.) I imagine young Isabelle was relieved.

PAULINA: He was most likely sending regrets to Spain when you saw him.

HERMIONE: I see.

PAULINA: Our Sicilia is trapped in stasis, overgrowth, and rot. It's not hard to understand why there is pressure to defy the oracle. But the danger in giving up—

HERMIONE: Aren't you tired of the burden?

PAULINA: I have faith that Apollo will restore us when he's sure we're ready. It's why I help Leontes build and rebuild your monument. We keep starting over—refining your features—the shape of your eye—a hand as you would have rested it. There's a light in him when we look back on you. I wish you could see it.

> (HERMIONE goes to the linens PAULINA brought. She touches them.)

PAULINA: (Pause.) The washing has been light.

HERMIONE: I've stopped bleeding.

PAULINA: No—you can't –don't tell me—it'll be my death— in the orchard? Have you? If there were another child—

HERMIONE: You think I'm—at my age—

PAULINA: I can't remember your age.

HERMIONE: Me either.

PAULINA: It's been so long—I could see—no, not you. You wouldn't—

HERMIONE: There will be no more heirs. Not from me anyway.

PAULINA: Oh. You've *stopped bleeding*.

HERMIONE: That's what I told you. What happens next?

PAULINA: I don't know. First, I'll bring red wine. (Pause.) You know the difference between loss and lost? Loss is permanent—people apologize to you for it. Lost leaves room for hope. If we're to right ourselves we have to—I don't know—In my prayers, I keep landing on the word grace.

HERMIONE: What if I have none to give?

PAULINA: Maybe now is the time for you to go to him.

HERMIONE: No—

PAULINA: The only heir is lost. We would be looking for her together—but how to present you—that's problematic—

HERMIONE: Please don't tell him.

PAULINA: Surely Apollo would grant us—

HERMIONE: Please. I won't ask for anything else. Please.

PAULINA: (Pause.) I won't.

HERMIONE: (Pause.) Do you think they're looking down on us right now—the gods?

PAULINA: I have to believe we're always in their line of sight.

HERMIONE: Is that why you keep buying all the paintings?

PAULINA: If you won't be needing anything—

> (She starts to exit.)

HERMIONE: I'm sorry. (Indicating the paintings.) They mean the world to me. And I miss the light.

PAULINA: Me too.

> (**PAULINA** exits.)

<u>SCENE VIII</u>

(Lights up on **DONNA** rifling around behind
a shelf in her kitchen. The **BEAR** enters. Real-
izing it's her and not **PERDITA** in the kitchen,
he attempts to exit.)

DONNA: Don't try and sneak away. I see you.

(The **BEAR** freezes.)

DONNA: I could have you trapped, slung up and dissected
for a year's worth of sustenance because of what you've
done to this place. Not to mention you ATE a man! But I
choose not to. I know what you're trying to do. It's her first
sheep shearing festival—I mean the first one where she's
going to solo—singing—dancing. Twelve years old, if we're
keeping track. She's going to shine and you want to keep
the lechers within arm's length. She's grown on you. You're
fond of her—just like the rest of us. But I can't have you
going after the lechers. Leave that to me. (Continuing to
search behind the shelf.) The old man tries to hide my bot-
tles, but he's not as sharp as he used to be.

(She pulls out a bottle.)

DONNA: Are you staying for a wee dram?

(The **BEAR** nods an emphatic yes.)

DONNA: I shouldn't reward you for your crimes, and you're
fat. But you've got me feeling sorry for you. And you really
do need to sleep. (She pours him a drink.) There you are.
Drink up and get on out of here. You're going to scare the
guests.

(The **BEAR** holds out his glass for another
shot. She reluctantly obliges.)

DONNA: (She pours herself one more.) That's all we're getting. I have to face people, you know.

> (**DONNA** puts water in the bottle and returns
> it to its hiding place. The bottle clanks against
> something hard.)

DONNA: What's this? (She pulls out an ornate box.) Gracious. It's the box what came with the child. So that's where he keeps it. I haven't seen it since he brought her home. I was told never to speak of it again.

> (She retrieves the box and opens it. She begins
> to examine its contents.)

DONNA: Oh Mr. Bear, would you look at this? It's a Sicilian charm. And do you see this lace? This lace is too good for a duke or duchess or courtier or even a bishop, but what do I know? Some woman worked until her fingers bled on this lace, but those royals hardly notice. My sister Miriam tells me all they talk about is the weather. And the queen's as dull as air.

> (She starts to put the lace away, but decides
> against it. Instead, she puts it in her hair
> and begins a performance for the **BEAR**.
> **PERDITA**, now 10, enters sometime during
> **DONNA'S** speech. The **BEAR** waves at her, but
> she doesn't see him, so he exits.)

(She takes on the persona of a queen.) It's a lovely day indeed. Yes. Mmmm. The breeze is—breezy. And the dew, quite moist. The clouds have a distinct puff to them. Mmmmm. I have heard—though I am not prone to spread rumors—but I have heard that just over the hill, there is a farm and every spring they have the most pleasant sheep shearing. I am told the mistress of the house—Donna they call her—not unlike MA-Donna—Ha—she arranges the entire feast. And the shearers—three-man song men all—they sing like angels. I would most enjoy going, yet I disdain *sheep*.

> (**DONNA** suddenly turns and sees **PERDITA**.
> The **BEAR** has vanished.)

DONNA: Oh.

PERDITA: Go on.

DONNA: I was—I just—

PERDITA: Did you buy that lace?

DONNA: I—ah—

PERDITA: It's so beautiful.

DONNA: I—had some Madera brewing—you know—fermenating—or fermenting—or whatnot in the—up on the—I thought it might be ready. It was behind this box. I thought you were feeding the chickens.

PERDITA: They're fed—

DONNA: Cleaning the shed—

PERDITA: It's clean. What's in the box?

DONNA: Not much really—It's Sheep Shearing Day. No one is idle on Sheep Shearing Day! Do something!

> (**PERDITA** goes to the box. She looks at the
> charm, and the linens. She picks up some
> linen and smells it.)

PERDITA: Look at this linen! How did we—

DONNA: Your grandfather—a long time ago.

PERDITA: A long time ago what?

DONNA: He—well, there were some sheep that got themselves lost. He and your brother went to the woods to look for them and they—they found this box—washed up on the shore.

PERDITA: Baby clothes—

DONNA: Yes.

PERDITA: For a royal baby it looks like—

DONNA: Absolutely.

PERDITA: Who died at sea—

DONNA: Most likely.

PERDITA: Creepy.

DONNA: Let's put this away now. You can help me with the rum cake. Your grandfather brought some of the most glorious raisins from town. They're golden! I'm surprised he made it back without getting hoodwinked—wasting his coin on trinkets. And we need to practice our song—

PERDITA: Can I put the lace in my hair?

DONNA: I have to put this away before he comes in and finds—

PERDITA: Just for a minute?

DONNA: Alright then. Turn around and let me weave it in.

> (**DONNA** weaves the lace through **PERDITA'S** hair.)

DONNA: Let me look at you. My. Isn't that something?

PERDITA: (Pretending, **PERDITA** curtsies.) Good day, my lady.

DONNA: Good day.

PERDITA: Fine weather we're having.

DONNA: Indeed.

PERDITA: The grass is quite—green. Mmmm.

DONNA: The greenest. Yes.

PERDITA: Have you heard about the sheep shearing festival across the way?

DONNA: Indeed I have.

PERDITA: Loads of fun, that's what I hear.

DONNA: Forget the sheep—it's the singing and dancing—

PERDITA: And the rum cake!

DONNA: Better than any you'll find in the king's court, I'll tell you that!

PERDITA: They tell of a girl there.

DONNA: Oh, do they?

PERDITA: They say she's not only fair, but a girl of letters—

DONNA: A girl of letters?

PERDITA: Does that mean smart?

DONNA: Absolutely.

PERDITA: She's a fair girl of letters who can dance a jig and carry a tune.

DONNA: And what a lovely tune it is. But I hear this girl, if she's not careful, will get a head so big it will roll off its shoulders from its own weight. Now give me the lace.

PERDITA: Let me untangle it first.

(**PERDITA** takes the lace out of her hair and gives it back to **DONNA**.)

DONNA: You'll tell no one of this.

PERDITA: Why not?

DONNA: Your grandfather's rage is why not. He thinks the fairies left this box.

PERDITA: Did they?

DONNA: We don't know.

PERDITA: Is it blessed or cursed?

DONNA: I can't answer that. Swear to me to keep silent about it, or I'll pull every ringlet out of your head, piece by piece.

PERDITA: I swear. You know that story you tell me—where the God seized the young girl and took her to the underworld?

DONNA: What made you think of it on a day like today?

PERDITA: Because this hidden lace is wasted beauty. Why didn't her mother fight harder to get her back?

DONNA: She did—it's why we have the seasons.

PERDITA: Her mother should've fought harder—then we'd have flowers all the time—like Nature intended.

DONNA: I've gotten stuck in the woods after the sun went down a time or two in my life. Feeling your way through the dark—after the branches scratch you up a bit—it makes you better appreciate the light. (Changing the subject, referring back to the box.) I'm going to be hiding this box in a place you'll never find—so you should just start forgetting—

PERDITA: But can't we take it out—just every once in a while—to look at?

DONNA: No.

PERDITA: Please?

DONNA: Don't ask me again. Now Grandma Donna needs a sip of her Madera. Would you like a little one?

PERDITA: No thank you. There are kittens in the barn. Can I take one inside to sleep with?

      (**DONNA** pours herself a drink.)

DONNA: No. (Pause.) Maybe once in a while when no one else is around I'll bring out the box. But you can't ever, ever ask me. Promise?

PERDITA: I promise.

DONNA: We'll ask a cat over from time to time for mousing. Now let's practice our song. (She clears her throat and begins to sing.) Rosemary and rue, a notable pairing.

PERDITA: Lavender and mint we delight in sharing.

DONNA and PERDITA:

Midsummer time Lady Marigold rises with the sun
And folds her flower when day is done
We're delighted you've followed her our way,
Weep no more, it's shearing day!

DONNA: Back to work.

(MUSIC. Lights fade.)

SCENE IX

(Lights up on **HERMIONE**, outside and alone
in the dark. She's been going out at night for
the last five years and she's used to it. She
sits. She breathes. She waits. **PAULINA** enters,
breathless. She carries two lanterns.)

PAULINA: I brought you some light. (She gives **HERMIONE**
one of the lanterns.)

HERMIONE: I thought you were right behind me.

PAULINA: I thought this might be a good idea. I've changed
my mind. We should turn back.

HERMIONE: Your eyes will adjust. Hold my hand.

(**PAULINA** grabs **HERMIONE'S** hand. They
make their way to an ornate statue covered in cloth. **PAULINA** removes the cloth.
HERMIONE stares at the statue.)

PAULINA: Ten years in the making. And re-making. Beautiful, yes? The marble came from Athens. This is a bad idea.
We should turn back.

HERMIONE: I want to read what it says. Bring your light
closer. (She reads.) *Here lies entombed Hermione faire, falsely
accused to be unchaste: cleared by Apollo's sacred doom, yet
slain by jealousy at last. What ere thou be that passeth by, curse
him that caused this queen to die.* Did you help write this?

PAULINA: I wish there was a moon. Then you could see the
marble—I never claimed to be a poet.

HERMIONE: Where's Mamillius?

PAULINA: We should leave before someone finds us.

HERMIONE: There's nothing here for him, is there?

PAULINA: No one can decide on a stone—

HERMIONE: After all this time?

PAULINA: I'm sorry.

HERMIONE: Polixenes said if he and Leontes had died as boys they would have entered heaven without a speck of guilt upon them.

PAULINA: And they would have died incomplete.

HERMIONE: My son was certainly incomplete, wasn't he?

PAULINA: This isn't the time or place for speculation. We should go.

HERMIONE: Where's Perdita? Is there a stone for her?

PAULINA: She's not dead.

HERMIONE: Where is she?!!!

PAULINA: She's not dead!

HERMIONE: How do you know?

PAULINA: I don't.

HERMIONE: It's been over fifteen years. I used to be able to feel her beside me. Now there's nothing. What if we have to accept the fact that she's dead?

PAULINA: We can't believe that.

(She goes to the statue and runs her fingers over her name. PAULINA stands beside her.)

HERMIONE: Do you know what? It's been a long time since I've heard someone say my name. It's strange to look at it.

PAULINA: Hermione. There I said it. Now let's go.

(HERMIONE steps up onto the base of the statue. She touches, then caresses the arms, the face, the neck, etc., as if saying goodbye to someone she used to know.)

PAULINA: For Apollo's honor. What's wrong with you?

HERMIONE: After I was arrested—after he *arrested*—Leontes came to me in prison—to my cell. He—he stood—he *lurked* in the doorway. Then he came in and sat beside me on the ground. In all my life I had never seen him sit on the ground. He touched my face. "There," I thought. "This is over." I touched his face. And then he—I thought he would hold me and—but he pushed me onto the floor—his hands—his hands were around my neck. *Whore*, he whispered it, *Whore*, and—and—and—pushed into me so hard. I still have dreams—nightmares—about his face. His hand over my mouth—his *face*—the rage—I couldn't breathe—and all I could think was that he was killing my baby—killing my Perdita—I left my body—floated above myself and prayed to Apollo to keep her alive. There were bites on my neck I tried to cover up—I felt such shame. I'm still covered in it. How can I ever go back?

(The two women regard one another.)

PAULINA: Clearly this monument will not do. We'll make something different. I'll see to it. Your neck—I thought it was—I didn't know.

HERMIONE: I can't stay here anymore.

(Sound of footsteps.)

PAULINA: Put out your light—

HERMIONE: Do you hear me? I can't stay!

PAULINA: Put out your light.

(The footsteps are almost upon them. They blow out their candles. **PAULINA** grabs **HERMIONE'S** hand.)

HERMIONE: I can't stay!

(They exit. The **BEAR** enters, sniffing slightly. He's gained even more weight.)

BEAR: What kind of a fetid place is this? The air smells like something dead. Take me back to Bohemia. (*He tears the head from the monument. Maybe he pushes the whole thing over. Maybe he examines the skull like Hamlet contemplating Yorick.*) You know, a baby bear will stay with its mother for about eighteen months. One good sleep, a bit of teat sucking and you're out. And you don't mate for another five years. Just grow. And eat. And shit. And grow. It's all a bit lonely, but pretty simple.

> (**PERDITA**, now sixteen, enters. She is dressed
> like a princess with flowers in her hair. She
> sits in a pile of daisies. She takes one and
> starts picking off the petals.)

BEAR: (*Referring to* **PERDITA.**) She doesn't see me anymore. Now I only appear in the delusions of an old, drunk shepherd lady and I'm knocking back too much myself. Look at me. If I could've stopped—if time could stop—I'd go back to about—no I can't go back. Still. I can't go forward. So much I wanted to say about—about what? (*Pause.*) The nature of man—small "m" man. There's one somewhere that's going to long for her so hard he'll think death less painful. *You're mine*, he'll say—in a thousand and one poorly written sonnets. And when he gets her—all that longing—maybe it won't mean so much. And then what? What is it with your lot and the illusion of *mine*? And yet—take Antigonus—I mean I did, and he didn't digest well—but here's something that took me a while to grasp. He ran *toward* me for *her*. For Perdita—a tiny human who couldn't even hold a conversation. Is that what your lot calls love?

> (The **BEAR** looks at **PERDITA** one more time,
> then exits. **PERDITA** continues pulling petals
> off of flowers.)

PERDITA: He loves me. He loves me not. He loves me. He loves me not. He loves me. (She picks up another flower.) He loves me. He loves me not. He loves me. He loves me not. *He loves me.* (Again.) He loves me. He loves me not. He loves me. He loves me not. *He loves me.* (Pause.) Fuck.

(PERDITA exits. **DONNA** calls out from her kitchen.)

SCENE X

DONNA: PERDITA!!!!! Folks are going to leave if we don't feed them and get some drink down their gullets! Where are you? I know you're in here. You're going to ruin the whole shearing. Disrespectful! Ungrateful!

PERDITA: (From off stage.) I'm not coming out.

DONNA: You will or I'll remove you with a pitchfork! I'm more than capable of it!

(**PERDITA** enters, still dressed like a princess.)

PERDITA: I look stupid.

DONNA: You look beautiful. Too beautiful.

PERDITA: Why can't I just be normal?

DONNA: That's not how it's done. This is your time. People are waiting.

PERDITA: I don't want it to be my time.

DONNA: For years I've prepared you for this—

PERDITA: Nothing is like it's supposed to be!

DONNA: Stop it now. What's gotten into you?

PERDITA: I don't know.

DONNA: Dumping on the ones who love you best in all the world!

PERDITA: This shearing is going to be a disaster—

DONNA: Like daggers to the heart to hear you say so—

PERDITA: I'M SORRY!

DONNA: (Pause.) Is the boy coming?

PERDITA: What boy?

DONNA: You know what I'm talking about.

PERDITA: I don't—

DONNA: Don't lie to Donna. I see everything. Is he coming? Is that the reason for all the *drama*?

PERDITA: (Dramatically) I'm not being dramatic!

DONNA: I know who he is.

PERDITA: You don't—

DONNA: Miriam tells me it's all anyone can talk about in the castle. She has to keep her mouth shut about what she knows. You're going to get all of us into some kind of trouble.

PERDITA: You don't trust me.

DONNA: I trust you to get us in a whole lot of trouble. That's the king's son—

PERDITA: He told me that he loves—

DONNA: It's the king's son, and if he told you anything else, he's a liar. He's interested in you for only one thing—

PERDITA: That's not true! He's brave and courageous, and—and—honorable—

DONNA: Will he honor a bastard child?

PERDITA: I can't believe you even said that!

    (**PERDITA** goes to her room and slams the door.)

DONNA: I'm sorry. Come on back out now. It's just—you're everything to me, child. And maybe you don't understand how much danger you might be in.

    (**PERDITA** re-enters.)

PERDITA: I was doing the planting last May and this bird—a falcon—I saw it go down in the field. It must've hit something—or had a battle with another bird. Before I could even get to it—the vultures were circling overhead. I picked

it up, wrapped it in a cloth, and suddenly he was there—
Florizel.

DONNA: Pompous name—*Florizel.*

PERDITA: I tried to reset the wing. And I gave the bird
arnica and other herbs—like you showed me. It lived and
they both kept coming back.

DONNA: I'm sure they did—

PERDITA: He said the herbs were magic—

DONNA: I imagine he did—

PERDITA: He said my eyes were like sea glass—

DONNA: Good God—

PERDITA: Oh Donna, he's a poet.

DONNA: A poor poet if he says your eyes are sea glass—

(**PERDITA** begins to cry. **DONNA** goes to her.)

DONNA: Shhh. Come sit by me.

PERDITA: He says he doesn't need to be king. He says he
can live—

DONNA: Like a shepherd? Do you see him wresting a stuck
lamb from a ewe's ass?

PERDITA: Disgusting—

DONNA: You've done it!

PERDITA: Tell me what am I supposed to do?!

DONNA: If Polixenes finds out—that could be the death of
us. They'll accuse us of witchcraft—

PERDITA: What am I supposed to do?

DONNA: We'll be hanged. Or flayed—tossed out on the ash
heap—old eccentrics like me don't fare well in this strange
new world.

PERDITA: I told him again and again this will end in disaster.

DONNA: I won't let it.

PERDITA: Will you help me?

DONNA: I'd do anything for you. (Pause.) He won't be at our shearing, so forget for a while if you can.

PERDITA: Actually—

DONNA: Don't tell me—

PERDITA: He'll be in disguise—no one will know.

DONNA: As a shepherd? Apollo help us.

PERDITA: You can't tell anyone.

DONNA: Why would I tell anyone?

PERDITA: Oh Donna—

DONNA: Head crushing. Boiling. I've heard sometimes they pour honey on you—head to toe—and release the bees. And then there's your basic drawing and quartering. I've heard they've left some on the rack still alive with their bloody insides on display like so much rope candy.

PERDITA: I'm so sorry.

DONNA: Ah. Don't be sorry. It's your time. We'll—well—we'll make do. Leave it to Donna. Wipe your face. Adjust your crown. There. Now come over here.

> (**DONNA** wipes **PERDITA'S** face and adjusts her flower crown. She retrieves the box of **PERDITA'S** baby things from a hiding place.)

DONNA: Do you recall this lace?

PERDITA: We haven't looked at it in years.

DONNA: Let's put a bit of it in with your flowers.

> (**DONNA** weaves the lace through the flower crown.)

DONNA: There now.

PERDITA: Do I look stupid?

DONNA: You look like an angel. (Pause.) You started walking when you were just a wee thing—around nine months or so. *Knock 'em down!* That's what the old wives say you should do if a baby starts to walk too soon. *Walking too soon makes them daft* they say. So I did. I knocked you down. But you'd pull yourself up again—your chubby little legs like springs. You'd laugh and laugh. It was all a game to you. And the first time you let go and began to move, you moved away from me. Now you go out and play the part you were destined to play. I'll stay here and push the food and drink out until it's time for the dancing. Then we'll fix some things.

PERDITA: Oh Donna—if it weren't for you, I wouldn't know anything. I love you.

(**PERDITA** throws her arms around **DONNA**.)

DONNA: All will be well.

(**PERDITA** pulls herself together. **DONNA** pushes **PERDITA** out the door.)

DONNA: Now go.

(**DONNA** puts everything back in the box that came with **PERDITA**. She closes it and sets it in front of her.)

DONNA: Sea glass. . .

(MUSIC. Lights fade.)

SCENE XI

(Lights up on **HERMIONE**. Her desk has been cleared. She sits in front of the fire. She is burning the letters she wrote to **PERDITA**. **PAULINA** bursts through the door.)

PAULINA: What are you doing?

HERMIONE: Removing every trace.

PAULINA: I have news—

HERMIONE: I have to go—

PAULINA: Listen—

HERMIONE: Let me go.

(**HERMIONE** heads for the door. **PAULINA** blocks it.)

HERMIONE: Let me out!

PAULINA: Shhh. Please.

HERMIONE: LET ME OUT!

PAULINA: Listen to me—

HERMIONE: I'm not your prisoner.

PAULINA: No.

HERMIONE: Then let me go.

PAULINA: Give me one minute. It's all I ask.

HERMIONE: I don't have another minute.

PAULINA: Please.

(**HERMIONE** remains silent. **PAULINA** continues.)

PAULINA: A ship arrived this morning. I was at the court with Leontes when they came. Strangers—from Bohemia—A young man, who claims to be Polixenes' son—

HERMIONE: Polixenes' son?

PAULINA: He's called Florizel.

HERMIONE: Pompous name. Polixenes' son?

PAULINA: He wanted to meet with Leontes and they brought them in. The moment I saw her I knew it. Our Perdita has been found!

HERMIONE: What does she look like?

PAULINA: Like the day you arrived in Sicilia.

HERMIONE: Terrified?

PAULINA: And radiant.

HERMIONE: Where has she been? Is she hurt? What does her voice sound like?

PAULINA: Antigonus left her in Bohemia.

HERMIONE: Antigonus?

PAULINA: They brought me his ring. See here. And this— his mother did the stitching. (She holds up a handkerchief.) The stories say he was consumed by a bear.

HERMIONE: A bear?

PAULINA: Quite an original death. I expected nothing less of him, and I am certain I will continue to grieve in my time, but right now, all is overshadowed by Florizel and Perdita who came to this darkness—for love.

HERMIONE: How do you know it's love?

PAULINA: How do I know it's not?

(HERMIONE starts to speak. PAULINA stops her.)

PAULINA: Listen. The boy with the pompous name tried to pass her off as a princess from Libya. I knew he was lying, but I held my tongue—

HERMIONE: Libya?

PAULINA: Let me finish. Polixenes has forbidden their marriage because he believes Perdita is a shepherdess.

HERMIONE: She herds sheep?

PAULINA: Among other things.

HERMIONE: Outside?

PAULINA: One doesn't herd sheep *inside*. Now we know who has raised her—

HERMIONE: I wonder if she knows how to dance.

PAULINA: She didn't mention it. Let me finish. Polixenes came in hot after his son—

HERMIONE: Polixenes is here?

PAULINA: And the old shepherd who helped raised her. There's so much more to tell, but the shepherd had the box and the charm and the lace that smells like you to prove Perdita is, well—yours! Ours! The bonfires are burning in celebration—

HERMIONE: Tell her I'm dead.

PAULINA: What?

HERMIONE: Tell her I'm dead.

PAULINA: You're overwhelmed—

HERMIONE: She has been loved. And she will be loved. How can I ever know her?

PAULINA: How can you not?

HERMIONE: What do I have to offer?

PAULINA: Is that a serious question?

HERMIONE: It's best for her to only imagine—

PAULINA: She doesn't have to imagine. When Leontes saw the pieces of his monument on the ground—the pieces of you—I thought he'd be full of rage but he said, *we'll start again, Paulina.* I told him to leave it to me—of course I said that. And every day I lied. I spoke of a master—Giulio

Romano—who was remaking you. Leontes told his daughter—our Perdita—of this phantom creation—this masterpiece. She wants nothing more than to see it.

HERMIONE: There's nothing to see.

PAULINA: (Looking directly at HERMIONE.) There's everything to see. (She goes to the painting.) Perhaps Giulio Romano *has* created you. It's not the likeness of dead marble—but something alive—extraordinary.

HERMIONE: Ordinary—

PAULINA: Both. We'll free the woman from the painting. (She goes to the *Madonna of the Cat* painting.) You'll put on a veil. You will be still and straight like a statue until your daughter touches you.

HERMIONE: And the man in the doorway?

PAULINA: You get to decide how far he can enter.

HERMIONE: I see. (Pause.) And everyone will believe I've been somehow resurrected.

PAULINA: Re-born seems closer.

HERMIONE: (She puts her hand on her neck.) I can't do it.

> (PAULINA looks at the letters that have not
> been burned.)

PAULINA: Then who gets to tell the story?

> (HERMIONE is silent.)

PAULINA: I—I'll keep the door unlocked as I always have. If I return and you're gone—I'll never speak about you again. If you're here, we'll proceed as planned.

> (PAULINA exits. HERMIONE waits a moment, then gathers up the remaining letters
> to burn, but the painting catches her eye. She
> sets the letters down. She goes to the paint-

ing. She touches it. She takes it in. She hes-
itates. She walks around the room, ending
up under the skylight. She holds her hand
up to the rain outside, but since the leak has
been fixed, none gets in. She goes to her desk
where a pitcher of water sits. She pours the
water on her head, as if she's baptizing herself. She takes the lace cloth from off of her
desk and wipes her face with it. Then she
drapes it over her head. She sits in the middle of all the Madonna and Child paintings
and waits.)

SCENE XII

(Lights up on **DONNA** alone in her kitchen
with her Madera. She wears a bit of **PERDI-
TA'S** lace. The **BEAR** enters.)

DONNA: You look like you're needing a wee bear hug. Come
sit by Donna.

(The **BEAR** sits by **DONNA**. She pours him
a drink. He takes it. Suddenly he's weeping.
DONNA strokes his fur.)

DONNA: Shhh. There, there. She broke your heart a little,
like all children do. I sent her off with the charm and the
lace. Most of it anyway. (She indicates the bit she's kept for
herself.) They'll know her when they see her. The old man
went too—to tell our story. Doubtful I'll see them again—
so it might just be the two of us. Ah, Mr. Bear. She was
never ours to begin with. But what we gave her—that won't
be erased. The girl knows how to put her hands in the dirt.
And the boy—*Florizel*—he's a little daft, but he'll be all
right. Our Perdita is a good girl, and a brave girl. But she
was never ever ours.

(The **BEAR** and **DONNA** drink. Exhausted,
the **BEAR** breaks into sobs again. **DONNA**
comforts him.)

DONNA: There, there Bear. You can rest now. We don't need
you shredding our visitors anymore, do we? There there.
Sleep now.

(**DONNA** begins to rock him like a baby. She
hums a lullaby until he stops weeping and
falls asleep. MUSIC.)

SCENE XIII

> (Lights up on **PAULINA**, **PERDITA**, and **HER-MIONE** as they are in the final scene of *The Winter's Tale*.)

PAULINA: Music, awake her; strike!

Tis time; descend; be stone no more; approach;
Strike all that look upon with marvel. Come,
I'll fill your grave up: stir, nay, come away,

Bequeath to death your numbness, for from him
Dear life redeems you. You perceive she stirs:

> *(**HERMIONE** comes down)*

Start not; her actions shall be holy as
You hear my spell is lawful: do not shun her
Until you see her die again; for then
You kill her double. . .

That she is living,
Were it but told you, should be hooted at
Like an old tale: but it appears she lives,
Though yet she speak not. (To **PERDITA**.) Mark a little while.
Please you to interpose, fair madam: kneel
And pray your mother's blessing. Turn, good lady;
Our Perdita is found.

> (**PERDITA** goes to **HERMIONE**. **HERMIONE** touches the lace in **PERDITA'S** hair, which matches the lace on her head.)

HERMIONE:

You gods, look down
And from your sacred vials pour your graces

Upon my daughter's head! Tell me, mine own.
Where hast thou been preserved? where lived? how found
Thy father's court? for thou shalt hear that I,
Knowing by Paulina that the oracle
Gave hope thou wast in being, have preserved
Myself to see the issue.

> (**HERMIONE** and **PERDITA** regard each oth-
> er. They touch hands and are frozen in the
> light. The **BEAR** enters.)

BEAR: It's the twilight of the gods, only nobody knows it yet. What will happen next? I don't fucking know. Maybe our story will live on. And maybe the man I ate will get another chance time after time—but I will take him out time after time for Our Perdita. Our Perdita—who is going to grow old like the rest of them. But at this present moment, I suppose she's what's next. And you can't take a bear who embodies time for granted! I've pinned her here in a moment of possibility. Would you look at that? (Pause. He regards **PERDITA** and **HERMIONE**.) I'm done. And I want you to—after you go on out into the good night with *your* little dramas and possibilities, I want you to know this: I'll be here—always with the last word—that I don't fucking—you know—pursue.

(The **BEAR** exits. MUSIC. End of Play.)